To: <u>Donald "Ronugua" Gunawan</u>

From: <u>Christina "Pei Pei" Duong</u>

Happy 25th
Birthday :)

A Birthday Wish for You

chris shea

J. COUNTRYMAN

Published by J. Countryman, a division of Thomas Nelson, Inc, Nashville, Tennessee 37214.

Project manager—Terri Gibbs.

Designed by The DesignWorks Group, www.thedesignworksgroup.com.

ISBN 1-4041-0364-3

http://www.thomasnelson.com
http://www.jcountryman.com

Printed and bound in China

To Angela E.
with gratitude for the cake,
the lei, and the unending
supply of support and
Kindness

For your birthday
I made a wish,

a wish that I could
fly

high up in your
birthday sky

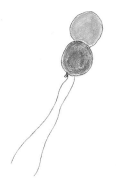

and leave your
presents
floating
by

in places that
would catch your
eye.

13

I'd
  tie
    a red gift

14

to a cloud

15

and a blue one

16

to a tall green tree.

And I'd
leave the
last one

18

on your roof

19

for
you
to
find

For me?

at the end

of the

day.

And every time
you saw one

22

as you went
about your
day,

23

it would float

down

to your

waiting

hands

25

and you'd find

a message

there.

The red balloon
would tell you,

in words I
chose with
care,

how glad
I am

30

that you
were born

31

and how wonderful

you make the

world

32

just by
being here.

The blue balloon

atop a tree

would waft down

on a breeze,

35

and then

you'd see

36

as you read its
note

just

how much

38

I think of you:

39

that you
sweeten life

like syrup

sweetens pancakes,

and you

soften it

42

like pillows
soften sleep.

The
Yellow balloon

I left up

on your roof

45

would bounce

gently

down
to your feet,

and you'd

pick it up

48

at your
birthday's end

49

and read

50

HAPPY BIRTHDAY

I made a
wish for you
today...

Read on →→

my birthday
wish for you:

51

I wish you

love from
family

and friends

53

in extraordinary

measure.

I wish you

peace
within

Your kind,
dear
heart

...Aah...peace...

that never
goes away.

57

But

most of

all

58

I wish you joy,

59

the
dearest
and
most
precious kind,

the kind
you've always
given me.

Happy Birthday To You !

63

Especially for

_____

From

_____

Date

_____

Member of the
Evangelical Christian
Publishers Association

Printed in China.

Life's Little Book
of Wisdom *for*
Women

BARBOUR
PUBLISHING

*E*very tomorrow has two handles.
We can take hold of it with the handle
of anxiety or the handle of faith.

<small>HENRY WARD BEECHER</small>

*Cheerfulness brings sunshine
to the soul and drives away
the shadows of anxiety.*

HANNAH WHITALL SMITH

I am only one, but I am one.
I cannot do everything, but I can
do something. And that which I can do,
by the grace of God, I will do.

DWIGHT L. MOODY

"Give, and you will receive. Your gift will return to you in full—pressed down, shaken together to make room for more, running over, and poured into your lap. The amount you give will determine the amount you get back."

LUKE 6:38 NLT

Nature's music is never over;
her silences are pauses, not conclusions.

MARY WEBB

Giving is true loving.

CHARLES H. SPURGEON

It is of immense importance
to learn to laugh at ourselves.

KATHERINE MANSFIELD

The great doing of little things
makes the great life.

Eugenia Price

Never be afraid to trust an unknown
future to a known God.

CORRIE TEN BOOM

The surest way to be happy is to seek happiness for others.

MARTIN LUTHER KING JR.

$\mathcal{T}$he sun will no more be your light
by day, nor will the brightness of the moon
shine on you, for the LORD will be your
everlasting light, and your God will be
your glory. Your sun will never set again,
and your moon will wane no more;
the LORD will be your everlasting light.

ISAIAH 60:19-20 NIV

$\mathcal{D}$o not wait for extraordinary circumstances to do good actions: try to use ordinary situations.

JEAN P. RICHTER

*We are the most appealing to others,
and happiest within, when we
are completely ourselves.*

Luci Swindoll

Better to be patient than powerful;
better to have self-control than
to conquer a city.

PROVERBS 16:32 NLT

If we had no winter, the spring
would not be so pleasant; if we did
not sometimes taste of adversity,
prosperity would not be so welcome.

ANNE BRADSTREET

*L*ife is what we are alive to.
It is not length but breadth. . . .
Be alive to. . .goodness, kindness, purity,
love, history, poetry, music, flowers,
stars, God, and eternal hope.

Maltbie D. Babcock

I am not afraid of storms,
for I am learning how to sail my ship.

LOUISA MAY ALCOTT

Do not forget little kindnesses,
and do not remember small faults.

CHINESE PROVERB

No one is useless in this world
who lightens the burdens of it for another.

CHARLES DICKENS

Character may be manifested in the great moments, but it is made in the small ones.

PHILLIPS BROOKS

"Do not worry about your life, what you will eat, or about your body, what you will wear. For life is more than food, and the body more than clothing. Consider the ravens: they neither sow nor reap, they have neither storehouse nor barn, and yet God feeds them. Of how much more value are you than the birds!"

LUKE 12:22-24 NRSV

There is no substitute for plain, everyday goodness.

MALTBIE D. BABCOCK

$\mathscr{I}$ have learned from experience
that the greater part of our happiness
or misery depends on our dispositions
and not our circumstances.

MARTHA WASHINGTON

$\mathcal{L}$ove is the divine vitality that everywhere produces and restores life. To each and every one of us, it gives the power of working miracles if we will.

LYDIA MARIA CHILD

It is not how many years we live,
but what we do with them.

CATHERINE BOOTH

Better a dry crust with peace and quiet than a house full of feasting, with strife.

PROVERBS 17:1 NIV

The smallest diamond is worth
more than the largest pebble; the lowest
degree of grace excels the loftiest
attainment of nature.

CHARLES H. SPURGEON

A soul cannot live without loving.
It must have something to love,
for it was created to love.

CATHERINE OF SIENA

*C*herish your visions; cherish your ideals; cherish the music that stirs in your heart, the beauty that forms in your mind, the loveliness that drapes your purest thoughts, for out of them will grow all delightful conditions, all heavenly environment.

JAMES ALLEN

Try to make at least one person happy every day, and then in ten years you may have made three thousand six hundred and fifty persons happy, or brightened a small town by your contribution to the fund of general enjoyment.

Sydney Smith

Therefore, as God's chosen people, holy and dearly loved, clothe yourselves with compassion, kindness, humility, gentleness and patience. Bear with each other and forgive whatever grievances you may have against one another. Forgive as the Lord forgave you. And over all these virtues put on love, which binds them all together in perfect unity.

COLOSSIANS 3:12-14 NIV

*Only a life lived in service
to others is worth living.*

Albert Einstein

He does most in God's great world
who does his best in his own little world.

THOMAS JEFFERSON

Finish every day and be done with it.
You have done what you could. . . .
Tomorrow is a new day; begin it well
and serenely and with too high a spirit
to be cumbered with your old nonsense.
This day is all that is good and fair. It is
too dear, with its hopes and invitations,
to waste a moment on yesterdays.

RALPH WALDO EMERSON

A kind heart is a fountain of gladness, making everything in its vicinity freshen into smiles.

WASHINGTON IRVING

When we do the best we can,
we never know what miracle
is wrought in our life or
in the life of another.

HELEN KELLER

You may say to yourself, "My power and the strength of my hands have produced this wealth for me." But remember the LORD your God, for it is he who gives you the ability to produce wealth.

DEUTERONOMY 8:17-18 NIV

All the beautiful sentiments in the world weigh less than a single lovely action.

JAMES RUSSELL LOWELL

$\mathcal{W}$e were not sent into this world
to do anything into which
we cannot put our hearts.

JOHN RUSKIN

Exuberance is beauty.

WILLIAM BLAKE

Two are better than one, because
they have a good reward for their toil.
For if they fall, one will lift up the other;
but woe to one who is alone and falls
and does not have another to help.

ECCLESIASTES 4:9-10 NRSV

Time, indeed, is a sacred gift,
and each day is a little life.

Sir John Lubbock

I avoid looking forward or backward
and try to keep looking upward.

CHARLOTTE BRONTË

*The beauty seen is partly
in him who sees it.*

CHRISTIAN BOVEE

The voyage of discovery is not in seeking new landscapes but in having new eyes.

MARCEL PROUST

But godliness with contentment is great gain.

1 TIMOTHY 6:6 NIV

Let there be many windows in your
soul, that all the glory of the
universe may beautify it.

ELLA WHEELER WILCOX

$\mathcal{L}$earn from the mistakes of others,
for you don't have enough time
to make them all yourself!

MARCUS AURELIUS

A child is the root of the heart.

CAROLINA MARIA DE JESUS

Live as if you were to die tomorrow.
Learn as if you were to live forever.

MAHATMA GANDHI

The LORD bless thee, and keep thee:
The LORD make his face shine upon thee,
and be gracious unto thee: The LORD
lift up his countenance upon thee,
and give thee peace.

NUMBERS 6:24-26 KJV

*Nothing is so strong as gentleness,
and nothing so gentle as real strength.*

Francis de Sales

The splendor of the rose and the whiteness of the lily do not rob the little violet of its scent nor the daisy of its simple charm. If every tiny flower wanted to be a rose, spring would lose its loveliness.

THÉRÈSE OF LISIEUX

The joyful birds prolong the strain,
their songs with every spring renewed;
the air we breathe, and falling rain,
each softly whispers: God is good.

JOHN HAMPDEN GURNEY

*I*s it so small a thing to have
enjoyed the sun, to have lived light
in the spring, to have loved,
to have thought, to have done?

MATTHEW ARNOLD

The mind controlled by the Spirit is life and peace.

ROMANS 8:6 NIV

$\mathcal{T}$here is a past which is gone forever,
but there is a future which is still our own.

F. W. ROBERTSON

*This is the miracle that happens
every time to those who really love;
the more they give, the more they possess.*

RAINER MARIA RILKE

$\mathcal{L}$ife begets life. Energy creates energy.
It is by spending oneself that
one becomes rich.

SARAH BERNHARDT

Be great in little things.

FRANCIS XAVIER

*L*ove never gives up, never loses faith,
is always hopeful, and endures
through every circumstance. . . .
Love will last forever!

1 CORINTHIANS 13:7-8 NLT

It is better to give than to lend,
and it costs about the same.

BENJAMIN FRANKLIN

*We are made to reach out
beyond our grasp.*

OSWALD CHAMBERS

The aim, if reached or not,
makes great the life.

ROBERT BROWNING

$\mathcal{T}$ruth is the beginning
of every good thing, both
in heaven and on earth.

PLATO

Even a fool is thought wise if he keeps silent,
and discerning if he holds his tongue.

PROVERBS 17:28 NIV

$\mathcal{R}$est is not idleness, and to lie sometimes
on the grass under trees on a summer's day,
listening to the murmur of the water,
or watching the clouds float across the sky,
is by no means a waste of time.

SIR JOHN LUBBOCK

*It is easier to build strong children
than to repair broken men.*

FREDERICK DOUGLASS

The soul should always stand ajar,
ready to welcome the ecstatic experience.

EMILY DICKINSON

*Give me a sense of humor,
and I will find happiness in life.*

THOMAS MORE

*B*ut seek ye first the kingdom of God,
and his righteousness; and all these things
shall be added unto you.

MATTHEW 6:33 KJV

*To accomplish great things,
we must dream as well as act.*

ANATOLE FRANCE

$\mathcal{W}$here the soul is full of peace and joy,
outward surroundings and circumstances
are of comparatively little account.

HANNAH WHITALL SMITH

*Let us not hurry so in our pace of living
that we lose sight of the art of living.*

Sir Francis Bacon

Everyone has a unique role to fill in the world and is important in some respect. Everyone, including and perhaps especially you, is indispensable.

NATHANIEL HAWTHORNE

$\mathcal{D}$o not boast about tomorrow, for you do not know what a day may bring forth. Let another praise you, and not your own mouth; someone else, and not your own lips.

PROVERBS 27:1-2 NIV

If one advances confidently in the direction of his dreams and endeavors to live the life which he has imagined, he will meet with a success unexpected in common hours. Go confidently in the direction of your dreams! Live the life you've imagined.

HENRY DAVID THOREAU

The world is the work of a single thought,
expressed in a thousand different ways.

MADAME DE STAËL

*An ounce of blood is worth more
than a pound of friendship.*

SPANISH PROVERB

A good laugh makes us better friends with ourselves and everybody around us.

ORISON SWETT MARDEN

"For I know the plans I have for you," declares the LORD, "plans to prosper you and not to harm you, plans to give you hope and a future."

JEREMIAH 29:11 NIV

By perseverance the snail reached the ark.

CHARLES H. SPURGEON

A gentle word, a kind look,
a good-natured smile can work wonders
and accomplish miracles.

WILLIAM HAZLITT

He turns not back who is bound to a star.

LEONARDO DA VINCI

The creation of a thousand forests is in one acorn.

Ralph Waldo Emerson

*L*et us not become weary in doing good,
for at the proper time we will reap
a harvest if we do not give up.

G<small>ALATIANS</small> 6:9 <small>NIV</small>

The best and most beautiful things
in the world cannot be seen or even touched.
They must be felt with the heart.

HELEN KELLER

*The riches that are in
the heart cannot be stolen.*

RUSSIAN PROVERB

If I take care of my character,
my reputation will take care of me.

DWIGHT L. MOODY

$\mathcal{I}$ hold it true, whate'er befall;
I feel it, when I sorrow most;
'Tis better to have loved and lost
Than never to have loved at all.

ALFRED TENNYSON

*L*ove is patient, love is kind. It does not envy, it does not boast, it is not proud. It is not rude, it is not self-seeking, it is not easily angered, it keeps no record of wrongs. Love does not delight in evil but rejoices with the truth.

1 CORINTHIANS 13:4-6 NIV

*I do not pray for a lighter load,
but for a stronger back.*

PHILLIPS BROOKS

*D*ost thou love life?
Then do not squander time;
for that's the stuff life is made of.

BENJAMIN FRANKLIN

*M*ake no little plans; they have no magic
to stir men's blood and probably themselves
will not be realized. Make big plans;
aim high in hope and work.

Daniel H. Burnham

How can a young person stay pure?
By obeying your word.

PSALM 119:9 NLT

If God sends us on stony paths,
He provides strong shoes.

CORRIE TEN BOOM

Courage: Fear that has said its prayers.

UNKNOWN

He is no fool who gives what he cannot keep to gain what he cannot lose.

Jim Elliot

The only basis for living is
believing in life, loving it,
and applying the whole force of
one's intellect to know it better.

EMILE ZOLA

When you were born,
you cried and the world rejoiced.
Live your life so that when you die,
the world cries and you rejoice.

CHEROKEE EXPRESSION

*God is able to make all grace abound to you,
so that in all things at all times,
having all that you need, you will
abound in every good work.*

2 CORINTHIANS 9:8 NIV

Joyfulness keeps the heart and face young.

ORISON SWETT MARDEN

Start by doing what's necessary;
then do what's possible; and suddenly
you are doing the impossible.

FRANCIS OF ASSISI

Forgiveness is the oil of relationships.

JOSH MCDOWELL

Before me, even as behind,
God is, and all is well.

JOHN GREENLEAF WHITTIER

*One generation plants the trees;
another gets the shade.*

CHINESE PROVERB

The eagle that soars in the upper air
does not worry itself how it is to cross rivers.

GLADYS AYLWARD

I do not pray for success;
I ask for faithfulness.

MOTHER TERESA

Cheerfulness and contentment are
great beautifiers and are famous
preservers of youthful looks.

CHARLES DICKENS

*H*appiness consists more in small conveniences or pleasures that occur every day than in the great pieces of good fortune that happen but seldom to a man in the course of his life.

BENJAMIN FRANKLIN

$\mathcal{B}$lessed are the peacemakers: for they
shall be called the children of God.

MATTHEW 5:9 KJV

God's help is nearer than the door.

IRISH PROVERB

$\mathcal{W}$here we love is home—
home that our feet may leave,
but not our hearts.

Oliver Wendell Holmes Sr.

$\mathcal{W}$hen I am afraid, I will trust in you.
In God, whose word I praise,
in God I trust; I will not be afraid.
What can mortal man do to me?

PSALM 56:3-4 NIV

"The greatest among you will be your servant. For whoever exalts himself will be humbled, and whoever humbles himself will be exalted."

MATTHEW 23:11-12 NIV

Once we've tasted being alive,
we can't go back to being dead.
Aliveness in God is addictive.

NANCY GROOM

*Hope is putting faith to work
when doubting would be easier.*

ANONYMOUS

*N*ever bend your head. Hold it high.
Look the world straight in the eye.

HELEN KELLER

*Of all female qualities, a warm heart
is the most valuable.*

CHINESE PROVERB

What does not kill me makes me stronger.

JOHANN WOLFGANG VON GOETHE

J urge you to live a life worthy
of the calling you have received.
Be completely humble and gentle;
be patient, bearing with one another in love.

Ephesians 4:1-2 niv

*Write it on your heart that every day
is the best day of the year.*

RALPH WALDO EMERSON

If you are humble, nothing will touch you,
neither praise nor disgrace,
because you know what you are.

MOTHER TERESA

Think. . .of the world you carry within you.

RAINER MARIA RILKE

*P*leasure is very seldom found where it is sought. Our brightest blazes are commonly kindled by unexpected sparks.

SAMUEL JOHNSON

A gentle answer deflects anger,
but harsh words make tempers flare.
The tongue of the wise makes knowledge
appealing, but the mouth of a fool
belches out foolishness.

PROVERBS 15:1-2 NLT

The fountain of beauty is the heart,
and every generous thought illustrates
the walls of your chamber.

FRANCIS QUARLES

*What I must do is all that concerns me,
not what the people think.*

RALPH WALDO EMERSON

$\mathcal{S}$he has achieved success who has lived well, laughed often, and loved much.

BESSIE ANDERSON STANLEY

The best things are nearest: breath in your nostrils, light in your eyes, flowers at your feet, duties at your hand, the path of Right just before you. Do not grasp at the stars, but do life's plain common work as it comes, certain that daily duties and daily bread are the sweetest things in life.

ROBERT LOUIS STEVENSON

*Little children, let us love, not in word
or speech, but in truth and action.*

1 JOHN 3:18 NRSV

Friendships multiply joys and divide griefs.

Henry George Bohn

There is no road to success
but through a clear, strong purpose.

THEODORE T. MUNGER

*W*ell done is better than well said.

BENJAMIN FRANKLIN

Do what you love.

HENRY DAVID THOREAU

*L*ove never gives up, never loses faith, is always hopeful, and endures through every circumstance.

1 CORINTHIANS 13:7 NLT

The soul is healed by being with children.

FYODOR DOSTOEVSKY

*The greatest satisfaction in life is achieving
what everyone said could not be done.*

CHINESE PROVERB

What lies behind us and what lies
before us are tiny matters compared
to what lies within us.

RALPH WALDO EMERSON

*Everything has its wonders,
even darkness and silence, and I
learn, whatever state I am in,
therein to be content.*

HELEN KELLER

*Give generously, for your gifts
will return to you later.*

ECCLESIASTES 11:1 NLT

The glory is not in never failing,
but in rising every time you fail.

CHINESE PROVERB

The consciousness of loving and being loved brings a warmth and richness to life that nothing else can bring.

Oscar Wilde

*Let the eternal Truth be
your sole and supreme joy.*

THOMAS À KEMPIS

*A*ll truths are easy to understand once they are discovered; the point is to discover them.

GALILEO

Flee the evil desires of youth, and pursue righteousness, faith, love and peace, along with those who call on the Lord out of a pure heart.

2 Timothy 2:22 niv

Jrue silence is the rest of the mind;
it is to the spirit what sleep is to the
body, nourishment and refreshment.

WILLIAM PENN

*Good actions are the invisible hinges
on the doors of heaven.*

VICTOR HUGO

To me, every hour of the day and night is an unspeakably perfect miracle.

WALT WHITMAN

*If you have knowledge, let others
light their candles in it.*

MARGARET FULLER

"I have told you these things,
so that in me you may have peace.
In this world you will have trouble.
But take heart! I have overcome the world."

Joнn 16:33 niv

$\mathcal{U}$se what talents you possess:
The woods would be very silent if
no birds sang except those that sang best.

HENRY VAN DYKE

Yesterday is gone. Tomorrow has not yet come.
We only have today. Let us begin.

<small>MOTHER TERESA</small>

*So, if you think you are standing firm,
be careful that you don't fall!*

1 CORINTHIANS 10:12 NIV

*E*very experience God gives us,
every person He puts in our lives,
is the perfect preparation for the
future that only He can see.

CORRIE TEN BOOM